CLARA'S ON THE CURTAINS!

Being a further misadventure of the Wickley Women's Guild as first recounted in "Her Grace Will Be Here"

by

ARTHUR LOVEGROVE

SAMUEL FRENCH

LONDON

NEW YORK TORONTO SYDNEY HOLLYWOOD

Basic fee for each and every performance by amateurs in the British Isles — Code D

ISBN 0 573 03352 8

Please see page iv for further copyright information

CHARACTERS

Mrs Mabel Claythorpe
Miss Clara Simpson
Mrs Iris Nicholson
Mrs Sonia Carter
Mrs Jeanne McGregor
Mrs Mavis Moffatt
Mrs Amanda Price
Miss Celia Lupton
Mrs Annie Craddock
Miss Shirley Craddock

The hall in which the production takes place is supposed to represent the hall and stage of the Wickley Women's Guild

Time – the present. About 6.45 pm on a winter's evening

CLARA'S ON THE CURTAINS!

The hall and stage of the Wickley Women's Guild. About 6.45 pm on a winter's evening

If possible (though it is not essential) a record playing "There's No Business Like Show Business" is heard before the house lights go down. It continues for a moment or two afterwards, then dies away. A moment later Mrs Mabel Claythorpe bursts through the centre gap in the curtains. Mabel is a large, middle-aged woman, domineering, with a booming voice. She is the Chairman of the Wickley Women's Guild and lets nobody forget it. She is dressed in a kimono and her hair is in a net

Mabel (*glaring* L *and booming*) Clara, will you please open these curtains!

Miss Clara Simpson enters L, *in front of the curtains. She is a twittering, nervous spinster of uncertain age. She is dressed in a jumper and slacks*

Clara (*very agitated*) I'm terribly sorry, Mabel, but you've only just given me this job. I can't open them, they're stuck.
Mabel Stuck? Stuck? You are stage manager which means that you are in charge of the curtains. Clara, as stage manager—unstick them!
Clara Yes, Mabel, of course! At once! I'm terribly sorry . . .
Mabel Clara, the curtains!
Clara Yes, Mabel.

Clara scuttles off L *and disappears behind the curtains, and Mabel goes behind them* C. *There is a pause*

Mabel (*from behind the curtains*) Pull, Clara, pull!

The curtains suddenly fly apart about six feet and reveal Mabel standing C

Clara (*off*) There, Mabel, I've done it. I've opened them.
Mabel (*booming*) Clara, come here!

Clara enters L *behind the curtains to stand beside Mabel, who pulls her through the gap so that they both stand* C

Tonight, Clara, the Wickley Women's Guild are presenting a variety show, plus a dramatic one-act play, to help raise money for the Mayor's appeal fund to preserve the town's clock tower. Through the industry of our members we have sold all the tickets and——

Clara (*eagerly*) I sold six.
Mabel —we are to be honoured by the presence of the Mayor himself and it is our intention, nay our duty, to present a performance worthy of the occasion. And we can't do that if ninety per cent of the audience can't see the show! Clara, will you please open the curtains so that the entire stage can be seen!
Clara (*turning and seeing the six-foot opening*) Oh dear! But, Mabel, I pulled, I really did pull!
Mabel This is no time for pulling. Heave, Clara, heave! Put some back into it.
Clara (*tearfully*) But I'm not the heaving type, Mabel. Can't you persuade Wilkins to do them as he usually does?
Mabel Because tonight of all nights he's suddenly decided that he is the scene shifter only, and he refuses, positively refuses, to do any other duties.
Clara But we haven't got any scenery!
Mabel Who is bringing on the chairs and tables and setting up the various items we need for the one-act play? Wilkins! Who is working the thunder sheet at the play's most dramatic moment? Wilkins! Who is pushing the piano on and off the stage six times during the performance at the insistence of Mrs Wainwright so that she can be seen playing the instrument? Wilkins! Who is managing the lighting throughout the show?
Clara (*quickly*) Wilkins!
Mabel Right! Do you want to overwork the man?
Clara (*twittering*) No, Mabel, of course not! But I do feel . . .
Mabel And who insisted on being stage manager? (*Pointing an imperious finger*) You did!

Clara I never! You said at the first meeting . . .

Mabel Rehearsal, Clara, rehearsal! Let us be professional, please!

Clara Well, whatever you call it, you said at the first one, "I propose Clara Simpson as stage manager, all those in favour, carried unanimously," and I haven't been allowed to manage anything except make cups of tea.

Mabel (*aghast*) You are to manage the curtains, the most important part of the show! How are the audience to know an item is finished unless you pull the curtains?

Clara (*tearfully*) But I wanted to *be* an item. I wanted to recite.

Mrs Iris Nicholson enters R *in front of the curtains. She is in her middle forties, gay, slim, and very attractive. She is dressed in a very smart dress and has a mink cape slung carelessly around her shoulders. She stands* R *surveying Mabel and Clara, who do not see her, with amusement*

Mabel Clara, we gave you an audition and you recited the only poem you said you knew, and after the first verse of "I have a little shadow that goes in and out with me" we decided that you and your little shadow would be better out than in. In fact, the entire committee, with the exception of yourself, realized that you were no Dame Sybil Thorndike.

Clara (*with sudden temerity*) Well, when you sing *Mad Dogs and Englishmen* you should realize that you are no Noel Coward! So there!

Mabel (*outraged*) Clara!!

Clara (*aghast at her temerity*) Oh dear! Oh dear!

Clara rushes off L *behind the curtains*

Iris She's right y'know, you aren't! And you shouldn't wear shorts and a toupee. They may give the appearance of heat, but you haven't the figure.

Mabel (*swinging around furiously*) I'll have you know, Iris . . .

The curtains fly to and Mabel is enveloped in them. She fights furiously free and stands in front of them

Iris (*interestedly*) Was that meant to happen?

Clara appears in front of the curtains down L

Clara Oh dear, they've closed again. I'm so sorry, Mabel . . .
Iris You pulled the wrong rope, dear.
Mabel That will be our biggest worry this evening, Clara on the curtains.
Iris But I thought Wilkins was on the "rag".
Mabel Well, he's not! Clara is.
Iris I hope that's the least of your worries. (*To Clara*) The other rope, dear!
Mabel (*furiously*) Clara, will you please learn how to operate the curtains. Good heavens, the show starts in just over an hour.
Clara (*horrified*) An hour? Oh, my goodness!
Mabel (*shouting*) Clara, open the curtains!
Clara (*now a bundle of nerves*) Yes, Mabel! Of course, Mabel! I'll really try. Oh, heaven help me!

Clara disappears and at that precise moment the curtains fly completely open revealing an empty stage which has only drapes

Iris (*gazing upwards*) Heaven certainly did!
Clara (*popping her head out from the corner* L) No, that was Wilkins showing me how.

Clara disappears again

Iris (*moving up stage*) I hope Clara proves an apt pupil.
Mabel Thank God, they're open at last. (*Turning up stage to address Iris*) Now, listen to me, Iris . . .

The curtains suddenly close again as quickly as they had previously opened, leaving Mabel alone in front of them

Clara (*popping her head round the side; proudly*) And that was *me*! I did that.
Mabel (*shouting*) Congratulations! Now will you please open them and keep them open.
Clara Yes, Mabel! Of course, Mabel! At once!

Clara again disappears and a moment later the curtains fly completely open once again. Clara's head appears once more

I did that, too!

Iris (*languidly applauding*) Darling, you will be the hit of the show.

Clara Do you really think so?

Iris Yes, apart from Mabel, of course.

Clara (*delighted*) Oh, thank you, Iris, dear.

Clara disappears

Mabel (*icily*) And what did you mean by that?

Iris That Clara operates the curtains in a most professional manner. She'll probably pinch the notices.

Mabel I meant that bit about me. I didn't like the way you said it.

Iris Darling, I meant what I said. Of course you'll be a hit. Apart from producing the entire show you're in eight of the variety items out of twelve in the first half. You can't be anything else but a hit, they can't miss you. Your name appears on the programme with such regularity it would take a dose of salts to shift it.

Mabel Iris! That is professional jealousy. Just because you are an ex-actress and insisted on producing the show . . .

Iris (*gently*) I was asked to generally supervise and produce the one-act play.

Mabel And when we didn't agree with your advice you flounced out.

Iris Correction! When *you* didn't agree and took over the entire production I made a dignified exit.

Mabel The remark you made when you did exit . . .

Iris (*giggling*) I always did like a good exit line.

Mabel It was vulgar in the extreme.

Iris Tell me, did you do what I told you to do with the show?

Mabel Iris!

Iris Obviously not! It's still going on!

Mrs Sonia Carter enters R *with a great rush. She is in her early forties, plump but attractive, and knows it. She is very fulsome and gushing in her manner. She is attired in an over-elaborate wrap*

Sonia (*dramatically*) Darlings, darlings! Tragedy, tragedy! (*Wringing her hands*) What shall we do? What *can* we do?

Iris We haven't the faintest idea until we know what tragedy has occurred.

Mabel Sonia, for heaven's sake, what's happened?

Sonia (*waving her hands dramatically*) It's Amanda, poor, poor Amanda! I went into the other dressing-room just now and you'll never guess. You can't possibly imagine the disaster.

Iris She really does build up the suspense. I can't wait for the next instalment.

Mabel (*shouting*) Sonia! What's happened?

Sonia Darlings, it's so shattering! She's lost her voice, completely and utterly.

Mabel Lost her voice? She can't have! I was only speaking to her ten minutes ago.

Sonia (*still full of drama*) But now it's gone. (*Flicking her fingers*) Just like that! What can we do?

Iris Institute a search party, it can't have gone very far.

Sonia Iris darling, how can you joke. It's tragic! It's a shattering disaster!

Mrs Amanda Price enters R, *a very pretty young newly-wed. She is tenderly escorted on one side by Mrs Mavis Moffat, a youngish woman; and on the other by Mrs Jeanne McGregor, who is slightly older. Mavis and Jeanne are in housecoats, Amanda in a pretty wrap*

Jeanne Mabel! Iris! Oh, Iris, thank heaven you're here.

Iris I just drifted along early to offer best wishes or condolences all round.

Mavis We need more than that. Do you know what's happened?

Iris We have been informed, with a wealth of dramatic detail, by Sonia.

Jeanne But what are we going to do? Amanda's voice just went. One moment she was speaking and then she couldn't.

Mabel Nonsense! No-one's voice goes just like that.

Iris I must admit yours never has.

Mabel (*booming*) Amanda! I command you to speak. Speak!
Iris And that's an order.

All eyes are on Amanda, who keeps on opening and shutting her mouth like a goldfish

Mabel Speak!
Amanda (*in a strangled whisper*) I—can't!
Jeanne (*frantically*) You see, she can't! Poor Amanda!
Sonia We daren't tell the others. Can you imagine the panic? Can you *imagine*?
Iris My mind boggles.
Sonia (*with a sweeping gesture that includes everyone*) It must be our little secret.
Iris My lips are sealed.
Mabel Don't be ridiculous, Sonia. How can we keep this a secret?
Iris It'll be difficult to keep it from the audience. Some sharp-witted member is bound to notice.
Mabel (*shouting*) Shut up, Iris! This is serious.
Sonia Serious! It's catastrophic, complete and utter!
Mavis (*frantically*) It's worse than that! Apart from items in the variety half she's playing the lead in the play.
Mabel (*taking command*) Don't panic! We have just over an hour. Right! First of all—a doctor.
Iris (*turning to the front*) Is there a doctor in the house?
Mabel (*shouting*) Clara, here! At once!

Clara scuttles on L *in a great flurry*

Clara Yes, Mabel, yes! I'm here!
Mabel Find a doctor! At once!
Clara Yes, Mabel, of course.

Clara turns and goes to run off L, *but suddenly stops and turns again with a little squeal*

A doctor? Oh, Mabel, are you ill?
Mabel Of course not. Amanda has lost her voice. Get a doctor and there's no time to be lost.
Clara (*in a panic*) Lost her voice? But what about the show?
Mabel (*shouting*) I'll attend to that! Clara, a doctor!

Clara (*even more panic-stricken*) Yes, Mabel!

Clara rushes off L, *shrieking*

Amanda's lost her voice!

Iris Bang goes our little secret. That's what I like about Clara, calm and controlled in any crisis. She'll probably return with the greengrocer.

Mavis She's only got to telephone.

Iris Nobody told her that. She's probably haring up the High Street by now.

Jeanne But what are we going to do? Don't you realize the show starts in about an hour?

Mabel (*striding back and forth*) Of course I realize it.

Sonia (*wringing her hands*) An hour! This is a crisis! But what can we do? (*Her voice rises tragically*) What?

Iris (*admiringly*) What a performance! Is she as good in the show?

Sonia But what can we do?

Iris Well, we can wait for the doctor.

Mabel For heaven's sake let me *think*!

Sonia Of course. Quiet, everyone! Dear Mabel, such a rock.

A pause, as they all gaze at Mabel

Mabel (*suddenly stopping*) Right! Let us consider the facts.

Mavis Consider the facts? There's only one fact. Amanda's lost her voice.

Jeanne And she's playing the lead in the play, apart from other items.

Mabel Let me think. I am the producer. Stop panicking. Her voice may come back.

Jeanne If it comes back as quick as it went it should be back now. Oh, Amanda, please say something, *please*.

Amanda (*a strangled whisper*) I—can't.

Iris What on earth was she doing when it went?

Mavis (*distractedly*) She was absolutely wonderful last night at the dress rehearsal, but she wanted to make sure so we were going through her lines . . .

Jeanne And for some unknown reason she dried a few times . . .

Mavis And then she suddenly lost her voice.

Iris Oh!

Mabel Right! Amanda obviously can't speak, and we are forced to assume she may not be able to . . .

Jeanne Oh, no!

Mavis Don't say that!

Sonia I can't bear it. But surely the doctor will be able to do something?

Mabel We all hope so, but we can't be sure so we must be prepared. Now, who can take over her part in the play? Even go on and read it.

Jeanne Nobody! You forget we're all in it except you.

Mabel Then I will have to take over.

Mavis
Jeanne } *(with horrified shrieks) You!!*

Jeanne But you can't possibly. You can't be serious.

Mavis The character is supposed to be young and attractive like Amanda.

Mabel This is an emergency. Somebody's got to do it.

Iris I must say it's rather like Tessie O'Shea taking over the part of Peter Pan.

Mabel *(turning furiously)* You keep out of this, Iris Nicholson. We'll only have to alter a few lines.

Mavis *(with a shriek of amazement)* Alter a few lines?

Jeanne *(likewise)* We'll have to practically rewrite the whole play.

Mabel *(shouting)* All we have to do is to tell the audience what's happened to Amanda and announce that I am stepping into the breach at a moment's notice.

Jeanne *(near hysteria)* If you think I'm going on this stage playing your mother you're mistaken.

Mabel You'll just have to make up to look older.

Jeanne Older? Older? If you're coming on to play an eighteen-year-old girl we'll all have to make up to look a hundred and ten.

Mabel *(highly incensed)* But the show must go on!

Jeanne Then it will go on without me.

Sonia But, darling, Mabel is so right. *(Dramatically)* The show must go on! Even tho' your heart is breaking . . .

Jeanne The only thing that will break my heart is having Mabel call me mother. We'll be a laughing-stock. When I say to you

—(*acting*)—"Sylvia, what is that wonderful news you promised to tell me?" What do you reply? Go on, say it!

Mabel (*booming*) "Mummy, I'm the happiest girl in the world. I'm going to have a baby."

Iris goes into hysterics

Jeanne (*triumphantly pointing to Iris*) There! You see!

Mabel (*furiously*) She's doing that on purpose. It's not a funny line.

Sonia (*doubtfully*) Of course it isn't. But, you know, Mabel darling, it did sound a bit—well, a bit—well—odd.

Iris (*still helpless with laughter*) It sounded gorgeous. Mabel, you must play the part.

Mabel (*really losing her temper*) With you in front—*no!*

Jeanne Thank God for that, because I'm definitely not going on to play your mother! And that's final! (*To Amanda*) Amanda, please, please, don't you see what a mess we're in? You've got to get your voice back otherwise we'll have to cut the play.

Amanda, near to tears, stands silent

Mavis If we cut the play half the show is gone.

Sonia But, darlings, she's in other items as well, and if we cut those . . .

Mabel I will not be beaten. Even though you're letting us down, Jeanne . . .

Jeanne Me? Letting you down? I'm stopping you making a fool of yourself . . .

Mabel (*highly incensed*) Make a fool of myself! I was saving the . . .

Iris As a paying member of the audience I am expecting to see a show—so what's going to happen?

Mavis (*suddenly*) Iris! Of course! Darling, we're stupid. An ex-professional actress you could help us out. You could read the part of "Sylvia". I'm sure the audience . . .

Mabel Are you insinuating that Iris having a baby would be more acceptable than . . .

Iris Oh, I'm sure the audience would accept a baby from either of us should we feel so disposed, but . . .

Jeanne (*eagerly*) Oh, Iris, you could help us out . . .

Mabel (*shouting*) Let it be firmly understood that as producer I will not have Iris in the show. After what she said about it . . .

Mavis But this is an emergency, Mabel.

Mabel But not as dire as all that. If she comes in—I go out!

Iris And as you've lost the one-act play, and Mabel's in and out of the variety show like a cash register drawer at a January sale—bow to your producer.

Mabel (*triumphantly*) Thank you! Now then . . .

Mavis (*furiously*) I think you're being stupid and unfair, Mabel.

Iris Darlings, time marches on, and you've only got an hour before the curtain goes up . . .

Jeanne (*sarcastically*) On what?

Mabel A show! God give me strength! How can I think with all these interruptions? Now then, Amanda, what other numbers are you in?

Iris If she's lost her voice how can she answer? Anyhow, as producer you should know.

Jeanne She's one of the "Three little maids from school" which is number three on the programme.

Iris That's easy, change it. (*She sings*) "*Two* little maids from school are we . . ."

Mabel You can't change Gilbert and Sullivan

Iris I don't see why not. I've changed Shakespeare in my time.

Sonia Darlings, darlings, please. May I make a teeny weeny suggestion?

Iris As teeny weeny as you like. We're all agog.

Sonia Darlings, I hesitate to suggest it, but to help out in this emergency, this tragedy . . .

Mabel For heaven's sake come to the point!

Iris But you would like to be the other little maid from school.

Sonia Darling, it's only poor little me trying to help.

Jeanne But there's more of poor little you than would fit the costume.

Mabel It could be let out. Thank you, Sonia. Now then . . .

Miss Celia Lupton enters L, *dressed in the uniform of a Girl Guide captain. She is a mannish, middle-aged woman*

Celia Heard that Amanda's lost her voice. Jolly bad show. Right!

Don't worry, the Guides are here!

Iris (*dramatically*) Thank God! The cavalry's arrived in the nick of time.

Mabel Celia, have any of your Guides got the needlewoman's badge, or whatever you call it?

Celia (*amazed*) Have any of them got it? They've *all* got it. My girls . . .

Mabel Good! This is an emergency. Get Amanda's costume for the three little maids from school number and do something so that it fits Sonia.

Celia Don't worry, I'll detail two of the girls. (*She takes a whistle out of her pocket, turns* L, *and blows a shrill blast on it*) Simpkins! Butterworth! To me! To me!

Celia strides off L

Sonia Oh, Mabel, I won't let you down.

Mavis But what about Amanda's solo number? She's singing, or was singing, *Climb every mountain*. Oh, Amanda, please have another go. Try and speak.

Amanda (*again in a strangled whisper*) I—can't.

Iris Now's your chance to climb a few mountains, Sonia.

Sonia Darling, I couldn't do that. But I could . . .

Jeanne Iris, please, never mind Mabel. You must help us out.

Mabel (*outraged*) Never mind Mabel? *I* am the producer.

Jeanne Well, produce something! The show starts very soon and we've lost half of it already. Iris, will you do something, please!

Iris The only solo number I could do, which is respectable, is my old audition piece from *Coriolanus*.

"Because that now it lies you on to speak
To the people; not by your own instruction
Nor by the matter which your heart prompts you,
But with such words that are but roted in
Your tongue, though but bastards and . . ."

Mabel What! I'm not having that language in this show with the Vicar in front!

Jeanne But it's Shakespeare!

Mabel I don't care if it's Ella Wheeler Wilcox! I didn't know what she was talking about, anyway.

Iris Neither did I, actually, but it sounded good.

Mabel We're not having that and we're not having you either, and that's final.

Mavis Oh, what are we going to do? Oh, Amanda . . .

Celia enters L *with an inch tape and a notebook and pencil*

Celia (*thrusting the notebook and pencil at Iris*) Right! Simpkins and Butterworth are unpicking the costume.

Jeanne But when the doctor comes Amanda may get her voice back and she won't have a costume.

Celia We'll sew it up again. Don't worry! Ready? As I call out the measurements write them down. (*She goes to Sonia and whips the tape around her bust*) Forty!

Sonia That's a lie!

Celia (*oblivious, dropping the tape around Sonia's waist*) Thirty-eight!

Sonia That's another lie.

Celia (*dropping the tape to Sonia's hips*) Forty-three!

Sonia (*indignantly*) And that's a bigger lie. Now look here, Celia . . .

Jeanne But don't you realize that whatever we do it will never fit her. We'll have to scrap the number——

Sonia We will not! Mabel said . . .

Jeanne —and her solo number. We've lost two items.

Sonia Mabel said I could . . .

Celia I say, lost two items?

Mavis And the one-act play.

Celia Bai Jove, you are in a mess.

Jeanne (*bitterly*) You're telling us! Now tell Mabel!

Mabel Now look here, Jeanne . . .

Celia Not to worry, not to worry. Two items to be replaced. Right! First of all the girls will come on and sing a jolly rollicking roundelay called *Camp Fire's Burning.*

Iris That'll be sensational, Celia. And what else?

Celia I'll recite a little number I did at the camp fire last summer at the Officers' Refresher Course week-end. Went down terrifically well.

Celia strikes a dramatic pose

"A bunch of the boys were whooping it up in the Malamute saloon,
The kid that handles the music-box was hitting a jag-time tune;
Back of the bar, in a solo game, sat Dangerous Dan McGrew,
And watching his luck was his light o' love, the lady that's known as Lou."

Celia turns to Mabel

That's the first verse.

Mabel And the last.

Celia But there's ten more!

Mabel We're having no light o' loves in this show!

Celia (*indignantly*) Do you want help or don't you?

Jeanne (*really frantic*) Of course we need help. The show's got to go on. (*To Mabel*) Why can't Celia recite about her light o' love?

Celia I beg your pardon?

Mabel Because it's not suitable. We're not having a bunch of hooligans whooping it up with their girl friends in this show. It's not respectable.

Celia Why not?

Iris The Vicar's in front.

Mavis But he's practically stone deaf.

Celia And the roundelay *Camp Fire's Burning?*

Mabel (*losing all patience*) No!

Iris You see, the Fire Chief's in front.

Celia (*incensed*) Then I take it you don't need the help of the Guides?

Mabel No! Only on the programme selling, that's all.

Celia (*snapping*) Right! We are only to sell programmes and only programmes we will sell. (*She takes out her whistle, turns, and blows it*) Simpkins! Butterworth! Down scissors!

Sonia (*shrieking*) But my costume!

Celia What's unpicked—pin up! And I hope you have enough pins, because when my girls start unpicking they work like billy-ho! We will now organize the programmes. (*Another blast on the whistle*) Rally, girls, rally! To me, to me!

Celia strides off L

Mavis (*losing her temper*) Now you have done it. I've never heard . . .

Jeanne (*frantic*) Do you realize what you've done, Mabel? Amanda, please, please! For heaven's sake try and say something. We haven't got a show without you.

Amanda (*a strangled whisper*) I—can't.

Jeanne Oh, Amanda, try! Look what's happening.

Mavis Oh, where's Clara with that doctor?

Clara enters L, *out of breath*

Clara Mabel—the—doctor isn't—there.

Jeanne Oh, no! Not there?

Clara He's—out on—an—emergency.

Mavis It can't be bigger than the one we've got here.

Clara Has—anything—happened?

Iris Nothing much. It's all been really quite calm and uneventful. Mabel has everything under control.

Clara Then there's—nothing—to worry about. Mabel is—so efficient.

Jeanne Efficient! She's upset Celia . . .

Sonia I was taking over one of the little maids . . .

Mabel You *are* taking over the little maid.

Sonia (*losing her temper*) But my costume's unpicked.

Mabel (*shouting*) We can pin it up.

Sonia I can't go on like that. Something dreadful might happen.

Iris But you said the show must go on even though your heart was breaking.

Sonia (*screaming*) There's a slight difference between a broken heart and a costume that's liable to disintegrate at any moment. I won't do it.

Mavis But, Sonia . . .

Sonia No, no, no! If it can be pinned up, pin it up around Mabel.

Jeanne Pin it up around Mabel? Look at Amanda and look at Mabel. Even unpicked it wouldn't cover her front.

Mabel How dare you! I'm not . . .

Sonia (*still screaming*) Mabel is so efficient she'd overcome that. I'm not going on! D'you hear me? I'm not going on!

Clara Oh, Sonia . . .

Sonia (*pointing to Clara*) There's your little maid.
Mabel Clara can't sing!
Jeanne Neither can you, but that doesn't stop you going out in the midday sun with all those mad dogs and Englishmen.
Mabel Now look here, Jeanne . . .
Jeanne No, you look here. We haven't got a play . . .
Sonia You haven't got three little maids . . .
Jeanne We haven't got Amanda singing her numbers . . .
Mavis We haven't got a doctor . . .
Iris But you've still got Mabel out in the midday sun.
Mabel (*furiously*) One more word out of you, Iris . . .
Clara Mabel! Mabel! Mabel!
Mabel Oh, my God! Now what?
Clara I can help out. I can do my poem.
Mabel Once and for all, Clara, you are not going in and out with your shadow. Besides, you are on the curtains.
Clara (*bursting into tears*) No, I'm not! So there! You can get somebody else to do the curtains. If you're so efficient you can do them yourself.

Clara rushes off L *then suddenly stops and turns*

And I only hope you know which rope to pull.

Clara exits

Jeanne Now to crown it all even if by some miracle we get the show on we've nobody to work the curtains.
Iris As far as I can see you haven't got a show.
Mabel (*shouting*) If you'd only let me think. (*Suddenly*) We can all do encores. That would help.
Sonia You never mentioned encores at rehearsals.
Jeanne Encores? I only know what I've rehearsed.
Mavis So do I, and it took me long enough to learn that.
Mabel Then you should have been prepared.
Jeanne Were you prepared for Amanda to lose her voice?
Iris (*glancing at her watch*) In a little less than half an hour a wildly enthusiastic audience will be clamouring to enter this hall to witness a much advertised entertainment. Just thought I'd mention it.
Mavis (*horrified*) In half an hour?

Iris That's when the doors open. After that you have half an hour to sort out any minor problems that may crop up, in between dressing and making up.

Mavis Minor problems!

Jeanne (*furiously*) We haven't got a show. Amanda's lost her voice, but Iris could have stepped into the play but you wouldn't have her. Sonia could have filled in as one of the little maids but her costume's unpicked because you upset Celia . . .

Mavis (*also furiously*) Yes! What did it matter if all those men were whooping it up with their girl friends! At least there were ten verses which would have filled in more time. And . . .

Mabel Listen to me . . .

Sonia You've upset Clara, so we've nobody to work the curtains.

Jeanne And why? Because you are so pig-headed!

Mabel (*with outraged amazement*) Pig-headed! *Me?*

Jeanne Yes, you! Minor problems! We can't possibly have any more.

Mrs Annie Craddock enters R *quickly. She is a large, middle-aged woman, as formidable as Mabel. She is accompanied by her daughter, Shirley, a girl of about sixteen, gawky, and wearing spectacles. They are both dressed in white coat overalls*

Iris (*quick on the cue*) Want to bet?

Mabel Mrs Craddock, you are supposed to be supervising the refreshments in the refreshment room back there. (*She points to the back of the hall*)

Annie Well, I ain't! I'm up 'ere!

Mabel Mrs Craddock, we have a crisis up here, and . . .

Annie Well, it ain't your lucky night 'cos you've got another one back there. (*She jerks her thumb to the back of the hall*)

Sonia Oh, no, this is too much. Agony upon agony. I can't bear it. Mrs Craddock, what has happened?

Annie I'll tell you what's 'appened. First of all, 'ow many people do you think will want to come tonight?

Iris Hundreds, but we can only accommodate two hundred and fifty.

Sonia We're completely sold out. Not an empty seat.

Jeanne And at the moment, not a show.

Annie Eh? What the 'ell 'ave you been doing? You've been rehearsing for the past five months. Ain't you ready yet?

Mabel Of course we are. There will be a show, I'll see to that. And there will be two hundred and fifty people present. Now what?

Annie D'you 'ear that, Shirley? Two 'undred and fifty! (*She repeats with emphasis*) Two 'undred and fifty!

Shirley (*wailing*) Oh, Mum, no!

Annie Oh, Shirl', yes! Mrs Claythorpe says so—(*with heavy sarcasm*)—and Mrs Claythorpe's never wrong.

Jeanne (*bitterly*) That's what you think.

Annie 'Ow long's the interval?

Mabel Fifteen minutes.

Annie D'you 'ear that, Shirley? Fifteen minutes!

Iris I've a vague feeling that it may be a trifle longer.

Mavis You're telling us.

Mabel (*shouting*) No, fifteen minutes.

Annie (*belligerently, with arms akimbo, to Mabel*) Then will you please tell me 'ow me and my Shirley can serve two 'undred and fifty people in fifteen minutes? Go on, tell me!

Iris At a rough estimate that's just over eight customers a minute for each of you.

Shirley (*in a piercing wail*) Oh, Mum, I'll never do it!

Iris (*helpfully*) Again, at a rough estimate, that's eight seconds per customer.

Shirley (*in an even louder wail*) Oh, Mum, let's go home!

Mabel (*shouting*) Will you please stop your ridiculous estimating, Iris!

Annie (*horrified*) Eight seconds for each customer! My Gawd, I can't serve a customer with a cup of coffee and slap a sausage roll on a plate in eight seconds!

Mabel Mrs Craddock . . .

Annie And some of 'em want sandwiches and fancy cakes as well. They're like a lot of blooming cannibals!

Mabel Will you . . .

Annie And on top of that I 'ave to give change as well. And why? 'Cos they all turn up with pound notes, and——

Mabel Mrs Craddock . . .

Annie (*overriding her*) —your old man is the worst of all. 'E always wants change out of a fiver for a sausage roll and a cup of coffee. It's a wonder 'e don't want it on a Diner's Card.

Either feed 'im up before 'e comes 'ere or for Gawd's sake see 'e 'as some loose change.

Mabel (*raising clenched fists in the air and shouting*) Mrs Craddock, will you . . .

Annie (*jerking her thumb at Shirley*) And I 'ave to keep an eye on 'er!

Shirley Oh, Mum, you . . .

Annie Daughter of mine she may be, but she was bad enough when we 'ad civilized money, but now we've got this new lot—she's 'opeless. She can't get it into 'er 'ead that a tenpenny piece ain't two bob! In other words, I want 'elp!

Mabel (*shouting*) But you've got plenty of help.

Annie (*shouting back*) Would I be 'ere if I 'ad?

Mabel You have! The Guides are helping you.

Annie Well, I've got news for you.

Mabel What?

Annie They ain't! They've just 'ad a lightning strike.

Sonia Oh, no! Disaster upon disaster!

Jeanne They can't have!

Annie They 'ave! Their shop steward, Miss Lupton, 'as told 'em they ain't on refreshments so they downed tools, or sausage rolls, as you might say, and left. Real narked, she was. It's a wonder she ain't left a couple on the door as pickets.

Sonia My dear Mrs Craddock, it was all arranged.

Annie Well, it's all been unarranged. They say she said—(*jerking a thumb at Mabel*)—that they were only doing programmes.

Mavis She's right, you did say that.

Jeanne (*to Mabel*) Now look what you've done. It's all your fault.

Annie Oh, I guessed she was at the bottom of it.

Mabel Now look here, Mrs Craddock . . .

Annie I don't know what you've been up to, but I couldn't make 'ead or tail of it. Something about unpicking a costume for a bloke named McGrew while a camp fire was burning. Even Vic Feather couldn't sort that lot out. I said, unpick 'is costume if you must, but not during refreshment time. Anyhow, I thought this was an all-woman show.

Jeanne Mrs Craddock, please. We're in a terrible state up here.

Annie And I'm in a worse state down there. I'm sorry for your troubles, but I've got plenty of my own.

Shirley (*wailing*) Oh, Mum, we've got to get help. When I think of all those people and only you and me I . . .

Annie Don't worry, Shirl', don't worry! If we don't get 'elp, as your shop steward, *I'll* call a strike and we'll both down sausage rolls.

Shirley (*brightening*) Then we could go to the pictures.

Iris What's on, anything good? I might come with you.

Mabel You can't strike, we're in enough trouble as it is.

Jeanne (*bitterly*) And whose fault is that? But we haven't got to worry because you are going to think of something.

Sonia Mabel, you've got to do something—anything! Everything is going wrong.

Iris Going? It's gone!

Jeanne Amanda, please, please try and speak.

Annie Wotcher mean, try and speak? We 'ad a little chat about an 'our ago when she arrived.

Sonia (*tragically*) She's lost her voice.

Annie You can't lose your "hobson" just like that!

Iris Yes, you can, believe me, you can.

Sonia Yes, please try, Amanda dear. (*Brightly*) Say, "Hallo, Sonia darling!"

Amanda (*in her strangled whisper*) Hallo—Sonia—darling.

Annie (*awestruck*) Blimey!

Jeanne Please, Amanda, you've got to try. If you could speak, half our troubles would be over.

Annie (*jerking her thumb at Mabel*) And if she lost her voice sometimes you wouldn't 'ave any troubles at all.

Mabel Mrs Craddock, I've stood about enough from you . . .

Annie That does it! Shirley, get your 'at and coat. We're on strike with the Guides.

Shirley (*excitedly*) Yes, Mum! There's a smashing film on at the Odeon . . .

Jeanne No, Mrs Craddock, please—no! Please wait! (*Boiling over*) Mabel, it's all up to you. For heaven's sake, the show is due to start any time now . . .

Mabel Of course it's up to me. Now as producer . . .

Jeanne As producer apologize to Celia and let her help out in the show, then the Guides will help Mrs Craddock on the refreshments . . .

Sonia And sew up my costume.

Mabel What!

Jeanne And apologize to Clara, otherwise we have nobody to operate the curtains.

Mabel Clara will . . .

Jeanne And come off your high horse and ask Iris to read in for the play, and at least we'll get a show on. Only for heaven's sake do some apologizing otherwise—otherwise—(*hysterically*) —I'll organize a strike, too!

Annie 'Ang on, Shirley, a miracle may 'appen!

Mabel I will not be dictated to. As Chairman of the Guild and producer of the show . . .

Annie O.K., Shirl', let's go! The age of miracles 'as passed.

Celia enters L

During the following, Iris quietly exits L

Celia Hallo, Mrs Craddock, glad I found you. Terribly sorry about a few minutes ago. I do apologize. Lost my temper. Jolly bad show. Forgot we should help other people at all times. Very difficult sometimes. But don't worry. The girls will be helping out with the refreshments, working like billy-ho!

Annie Well, that's real 'andsome of you Miss Lupton. Ta a lot. Shirley, back to the sausage rolls.

Shirley (*wailing*) Oh, Mum, I thought we were going to the Odeon.

Annie We'll go tomorrow night. Come on! (*She turns to Mabel and jerks her thumb at Celia*) She's saved your bacon. Your two 'undred and fifty may not get much of a show, but blimey, they'll get some grub. But if you see your old man beforehand, for Gawd's sake give 'im the price of a coffee and a sausage roll.

Annie exits R *with Shirley*

Mabel That's settled. Now then . . .

Mavis But not by you.

Jeanne And we still haven't got a show.

Celia Right, I'll be off. Must get the girls organized with the programmes and refreshments.

Celia turns to go off L

Jeanne Celia, please—wait! (*To Mabel*) Mabel, time's running out.

Mabel gazes at them all

Mabel (*finally beaten*) Oh, Celia, that recitation. What's it called?
Celia "The Shooting of Dan McGrew."
Sonia Oh dear, does he die?
Celia (*cheerfully*) Oh, yes!

Celia strikes a dramatic pose

"Then I ducked my head, and the lights went out, and two guns blazed in the dark;
And a woman screamed, and the lights went up, and two men lay stiff and stark;
Pitched on his head, and pumped full of lead, was Dangerous Dan McGrew."
(*Cheerfully relaxing*) And you can't be deader than that.
Sonia But who was the other man?
Mabel (*hastily*) I'm sure we'll find that out later this evening if Celia will be kind enough to render the whole poem.
Celia Delighted! Only too pleased to help out. And how about that jolly, rollicking roundelay from the girls?
Mabel Anything, anything! We'd love it!
Jeanne Oh, thank you, Celia, thank you. I knew that . . .

Iris enters L, *in a rush*

Iris (*dramatically*) Amanda! Amanda!

Amanda swings round and Iris seizes her by the arms

There's just been a telephone call. It was your husband. Not to worry but your house is on fire.

Amanda shrieks, then speaks in her normal voice

Amanda My house! On fire! My God, what's happened?
Iris (*bursting out laughing*) Nothing, except your voice has come back. Keep calm, darling, your house isn't on fire.

Amanda It really isn't?

Iris Would I be laughing if it was? Relax, darling, relax, and realize your voice has come back. You're talking.

Jeanne Oh, Amanda, how wonderful! You're all right!

Mavis It's marvellous! Marvellous!

Sonia But what happened?

Iris Hysterical aphonia! In other words, an attack of sheer nerves. Going through her lines she forgot them a few times, got panicky, and lost her voice. I had it once on an opening night when I was in the West End, so I knew the symptoms. It only needed a shock to make it come back.

Mabel Thank you, Iris. I . . .

Iris We've had enough drama, now for Pete's sake go and get changed and inflict some of it on the audience! You've got a show to put on.

Amanda Iris darling, bless you! (*She flings her arms around Iris*) Of course I know my lines. I know them backwards.

Iris Well, do say them forwards, otherwise you'll confuse the audience.

Celia I say, in that case you won't need our help in the show.

Mabel Well, no, Celia, but we are extremely grateful and . . .

Celia Don't mention it. Jolly glad Amanda's O.K.

Iris Celia, do please blow that whistle of yours and get Simpkins and Butterworth working like billy-ho putting that costume together.

Celia Bai Jove yes, forgotten that! (*She gives a blast on the whistle*) Simpkins! Butterworth! To me, to me!

Celia strides off L

Sonia Oh, darlings, isn't it wonderful! Now the show can really go on!

Mabel Right! Let's get ready. Sharp's the word!

Clara enters L, *very agitated*

Clara Mabel! Everyone!

Mabel Clara, the curtains. Everything's all right now. The show will go on.

Clara It can't! It can't!

Mabel (*shouting*) What do you mean, it can't?

Clara You know I went for the doctor and he was out on an emergency call.

Sonia But what's that got to do with us?

Clara He was with Mrs Wainwright.

Mabel But she's our pianist!

Clara (*wailing*) She was! She's sprained her wrist and won't be able to play tonight.

Sonia Oh, darlings, right at the end, tragedy strikes again. This show is fated.

Mavis Oh, no! But what's going to happen to all the musical numbers?

Jeanne We'll just have to do without the piano accompaniment. And I'll sound ghastly.

Iris (*resignedly*) I knew I'd get raked into this damn show somehow. Don't worry, I'll tickle the ivories for you. Now for heaven's sake, go and get ready!

Mabel (*suddenly grasping Iris's hands*) Iris, bless you! (*She turns and looks out front, and a look of horror comes over her face*) Look! The audience! They're coming in!

With shrieks, they all run off R *with the exception of Iris, who stands nonchalantly up* C

(*Off*) Clara, the curtains! They work from the other side. Get over there!

Clara suddenly scuttles across the stage from R *to* L, *with a frantic glance at the audience*

Iris watches her entrance and exit with amusement

Clara (*off*) Oh, dear, they're stuck! (*Frantically*) Mabel! They're stuck! They won't move!

Iris The other rope, dear, the other rope. Gently, now. Gently.

Faintly we hear again "There's No Business Like Show Business", and the curtains very slowly begin to close. Iris smiles sweetly towards the audience

Good evening, Mr Mayor! Mayoress! We do hope you will enjoy the show.

Iris is lost to sight by the final closing of the curtains, as the music rises and—

the PLAY *concludes*

The cast, excepting Clara, take up positions behind the curtains ready to take a bow. The curtains open, presumably operated by Clara, who immediately rushes on and takes up her position somewhere in the line, looking very pleased with her achievement. After the applause, Clara rushes off again to close the curtains. This may be repeated

FURNITURE AND PROPERTY LIST

On stage: Nil

Off stage: Inch tape, notebook, pencil (**Celia**)

Personal: **Celia** whistle
Iris: watch

LIGHTING PLOT

Property fittings required: nil
A bare stage

To open: General overall lighting
No cues

EFFECTS PLOT

Cue 1	Before CURTAIN rises *"There's No Business Like Show Business" record: continue until start of dialogue*	(Page 1)
Cue 2	"Gently, now. Gently." *Restart record: continue until end of play*	(Page 24)

Lightning Source UK Ltd.
Milton Keynes UK
UKHW021831040820
367696UK00008B/338

9 780573 033520